THE
COUNTRY SPORTSMAN'S
QUOTATION BOOK

The
Country Sportsman's
Quotation Book

A *Sporting Companion*

Edited by
MARCELLE PITT

ROBERT HALE · LONDON

ISBN 0 7090 4632 4

Robert Hale Limited
Clerkenwell House
Clerkenwell Green
London EC1R 0HT

Photoset in North Wales by
Derek Doyle & Associates, Mold, Clwyd.
Printed and bound by
Bookbuilders Ltd, Hong Kong

To
Jack

Preface

From my earliest years I was brought up with stories of country sports. My mother used to hunt with the Pytchley and was an excellent shot, graduating from rooks in Devonshire to alligators in India. My father, who once rode from Dover to King's Lynn in Norfolk, was in his Territorial Army days with a mounted Company of bright young barristers – they called themselves The Devil's Own – where it was obligatory to be able to jump three horses at once over a hedge.

But I was born in London. It was not until I married and went to live in the Border Country of Northumberland, that I saw to a full extent the thrill and challenge of country sports.

I have much enjoyed putting together this collection of some of my favourite quotations, and widening my horizons with many new ones.

I hope that all lovers of field sports, whether about to take an active part in their favourite occupations or enjoying in memory from their firesides, will find something which will give them as much pleasure, in reading this collection, as I have had in putting it together.

I would like to express my thanks to the following copyright holders who have granted permission to include certain quotations: The Bodley Head, *The Daily Telegraph*, David & Charles plc, Faber & Faber Ltd, HarperCollins, Michael Joseph Ltd, SAIGA Publishing Co. Ltd, Longmans, Barry Hines, R.W.F. Poole, Douglas Sutherland and Peter Wheat.

MARCELLE PITT

There is a passion for hunting something deeply implanted in the human breast.

CHARLES DICKENS
Oliver Twist

'Unting is all that's worth living for – all time is lost wot is not spent in 'unting – it is like the hair we breathe – if we have it not we die – it's the sport of kings, the image of war without its guilt, and only five-and-twenty per cent of its danger.

R.S. SURTEES
Handley Cross

It isn't mere convention. Everyone can see that the people who hunt are the right people and the people who don't are the wrong ones.

> GEORGE BERNARD SHAW
> *Heartbreak House*

Hunting is not a proper employment for a thinking man.

> JOSEPH ADDISON

Tell me a man's a fox-hunter, and I loves him at once.

> R.S. SURTEES
> *Hillingdon Hall*

The English country gentleman galloping after a fox – the unspeakable in full pursuit of the uneatable.

> OSCAR WILDE
> *A Woman of No Importance*

A swimmer does not plunge into the seas at Dover because he thinks that it is the easiest or safest way of reaching France. The fox hunter is not chasing his dinner. Sport is independent of results. It is a perennial thing.

> STANLEY SNAITH

He [Mr Justice Roche] was, in very truth, a hunting judge, hunting whenever a list of his collapsed ... I had no serious falls, though there was one grim day when both judge and his marshal sat beside each other on the bench, each with a black eye of startling proportions.

> LORD HAILSHAM
> *A Sparrow's Flight*

For what were all these country patriots born?
To hunt, and vote, and raise the price of corn?
> LORD BYRON
> *The Age of Bronze*

Most of their discourse was about hunting, in a dialect I understand very little.

> SAMUEL PEPYS
> *Diary, 22 November 1663*

Hunting is one of the most sensual of pleasures by which the powers of the body are strongly exerted, but those of the mind remain unemployed.

> THOMAS ADAMS (d. 1620)

The dusky night rides down the sky,
And ushers in the morn;
The hounds all join in glorious cry,
The huntsman winds his horn,
And a-hunting we will go.
> HENRY FIELDING
> 'A-Hunting We Will Go'

Without foxes there would be no fox-hunting and without fox-hunting many would find it impossible to live through an English winter.

ANON

… he felt the glory of going fast,
Till the terror of death, though there indeed,
Was lulled for a while by his pride of speed.

JOHN MASEFIELD
Reynard the Fox

I have known a fox that was absolutely devoted to fox-hunting … after we had hunted him many seasons I regret to say we killed him.

MICHAEL BATEMAN

I am convinced that if a fox could vote, he would vote Tory.

a letter to the *Sussex Express*

If foxes, like women, had a vote I think they would vote unanimously for the keeping of fox hunting.
MICHAEL BATEMAN

A fine figure of a woman she was, they all agreed, as she sailed over the fences in her tall hat and perfectly fitting black habit with a bunch of violets in her button-hole.
SIEGFRIED SASSOON
Memoirs of a Fox-Hunting Man

Dauntlessly tenacious of life, she followed the Heythrop hounds over their hedge and stone wall country in Oxfordshire well into her eighties.
OBITUARY OF JOAN FLEMING
aunt by marriage of Peter and Ian Fleming
Sunday Telegraph, 1991

That the world is out of balance and lopsided we know
without being reminded of it by the side-saddle.
LORD BRABAZON OF TARA

The fox, when caught, is worth nothing: he is followed for
the pleasure of following.
REVD SYDNEY SMITH

D' ye ken John Peel with his coat so gay?
D' ye ken John Peel at the break of day?
D' ye ken John Peel when he's far far away
With his hounds and his horn in the morning?

'Twas the sound of his horn brought me from my bed,
And the cry of his hounds, has he oftimes led;
For Peel's view-hollo would waken the dead,
Or the fox from his lair in the morning.
JOHN WOODCOCK GRAVES
'John Peel', 1832

It is nought good a slepyng hound to wake.
GEOFFREY CHAUCER
Troilus and Criseyde

While the cock with lively din
Scatters the rear of darkness thin,
And to the stack, or the barn door,
Stoutly struts his dames before,
Oft list'ning how the hounds and horn
Cheerly rouse the slumb'ring morn.
JOHN MILTON
L'Allegro

He cast off his friends as a huntsman his pack,
For he knew when he pleased he could whistle them
  back.
OLIVER GOLDSMITH

Then drink, puppy, drink, and let ev'ry puppy drink,
That is old enough to lap and to swallow;
For he'll grow into a hound, so we'll pass the bottle
  round,
And merrily we'll whoop and we'll holloa.
GEORGE JOHN WHITE-MELVILLE
chorus of 'Drink Puppy Drink'

He had a warm heart for any horse in the world, and, like
every good groom, would sit up all night with a hunter
rather than risk leaving a thorn in one of its legs after a
day's hunting.
SIEGFRIED SASSOON
Memoirs of a Fox-Hunting Man

16

I like the hunting of the hare
Better than that of the fox.
WILFRID BLUNT
'The Old Squire'

I have heard it said of the 'backwoods' peer that he had three qualities. He knew how to kill a fox, he knew how to get rid of a bad tenant, and he knew how to discard an unwanted mistress. A man who possesses these three qualities would certainly have something to contribute to the work of the House.

LORD WINSTER
in a speech to the House of Lords

He who hunts two hares leaves one and loses one.
CHINESE PROVERB

How every nerve the greyhound's stretch displays
The hare, preventing in her airy maze.
THOMAS TICKELL (1686–1740)

I have known people who decided against buying a Mercedes because they reckoned the seats were about as hard – and as comfortable – as a hunting saddle.
STUART MARSHALL

If some animals are good at hunting and others are suitable for hunting, then the Gods must clearly smile on hunting.
ARISTOTLE

He shouted, 'I've got'n,' as his father had shouted in the church door during a sermon half a century before, calling the men to leave and pursue the tracks of a fox through the snow.
HENRY WILLIAMSON
Tarka the Otter

The stars grew bright in the winter sky,
The wind came keen with a tang of frost,
The brook was troubled for new things lost,
The copse was happy for old things found,
The fox came home and he went to ground.
JOHN MASEFIELD
Reynard the Fox

I am alarmed to learn from your leading article today that the Duke of Beaufort rides in a car bearing the registration number MFH 1. At these works we travel in Fox 1. May I be assured that, should we happen to meet his Grace on the road, no unseemly incident will occur?
H.P. FORDER
of Samuel Fox & Co. Ltd, in a letter to *The Times*

Here's a health to every sportsman, be he stableman or lord,
If his heart be true I care not what his pocket may afford.
ADAM L. GORDON

My hoarse sounding horn invites thee to the chase, the Sport of Kings.
WILLIAM SOMERVILLE

It's of three jovial huntsmen, and a-hunting they did go.
And they hunted, and they holloed, and they blew their horns also,
Look ye there!
OLD ENGLISH BALLAD

I have often observed in women of her type a tendency to regard all athletics as inferior forms of fox-hunting.

> EVELYN WAUGH
> *Decline and Fall*

'Unting fills my thoughts by day, and many a good run I have in my sleep. Many a dig in the ribs I gives Mrs J when I think they are running into the warmint (renewed cheers). No man is fit to be called a sportsman wot doesn't kick his wife out of bed on a haverage once in three weeks.

> R.S. SURTEES
> *Handley Cross*

Three things I never lends – my 'oss, my wife, and my name.

> R.S. SURTEES
> *Hillingdon Hall*

It is very strange, and very melancholy, that the paucity of human pleasures should persuade us ever to call hunting one of them.

SAMUEL JOHNSON

Racing and hunting excite man's heart to madness.

LAO-TZU, *c.* 600 BC

A sportsman is a fellow who, every now and then, simply has to go out and kill something.

STEPHEN LEACOCK

Hunting is fit recreation for a Pope.

POPE PIUS V

There can be no more important kind of information than the exact knowledge of a man's own country; and for this as well as for more general reasons of pleasure and advantage, hunting with hounds and other kinds of sports should be pursued by the young.

PLATO

The first pursuit that a young man just out of boyhood should take up is hunting, and afterwards, he should go on to other branches of education.

XENOPHON

I hate all blood sports involving animals whose panting death provides a thrill for the pursuers. But at least those who hunt the fox and the noble stag do put their own limbs at some risk.

PETER WILSON

The fox knows much, but more he that catcheth him.
PROVERB

He that will get the better of a fox must rise early.
FRENCH PROVERB

Fox hunting is a kind of warfare, its uncertainties, its fatigues, its difficulties, and its dangers, render it interesting above all other diversions.
PETER BECKFORD
Master of Foxhounds 1740–1811

A Master of Foxhounds to be perfect, must embody all the virtues of a saint with the commanding genius of a Kitchener, and the tact of a diplomat.
CAPTAIN J. OTHO PAGET
The Field Magazine

A hunter needs to be tireless, tubeless, able to gallop on; but more important stop, and find out where are the best gaps, lanes and pubs which open outside licensing hours.
RINTOUL BOOTH

Hunting is an occupation in which the incidents are as much a part of the object as the final result; everything about it, from the kind of clothes worn to the manner of the weapon used, enhances, in some degree, the hunter's plesure.
LEWIS MUMFORD

No one knows how ungentlemanly he can look, until he
has seen himself in a shocking bad hat.

> R.S. SURTEES
> *Mr Facey Romford's Hounds*

Men have deep-rooted instincts that prompt them to go out
and hunt. If they can't, look out for trouble ... Look out for
all sorts of violence and anti-social behaviour.

> RICHARD WALKER
> *Dick Walker's Angling*

Of all the creatures that were made he [man] is the most
detestable ... He is the only creature that inflicts pain for
sport, knowing it to be pain.

> MARK TWAIN
> *Autobiography*

Wild animals never kill for sport. Man is the only one to whom the torture and death of his fellow-creatures is amusing in itself.

    J.A. FROUDE
    Oceana, 1886

The fox's hunting is quite as legitimate and a great deal more necessary to his existence than that of the game-keeper.

    KONRAD LORENZ
    Austrian behavioural physiologist

The creatures that want to live a life of their own, we call wild. If wild, then no matter how harmless, we treat them as outlaws, and those of us who are specially well brought up shoot them for fun.

    CLARENCE DAY
    This Simian World

Blood sports are the only method that I know that controls the numbers of a species, especially predators themselves, without endangering their continued existence as a form of wildlife.

LORD HAILSHAM
A Sparrow's Flight

Sitting is but one thing in horsemanship and there are thousands of things in the art. I never knew in my life a good horseman thrown, but I have known many presumptuous, ignorant fellows get falls, for it is a mistake as ridiculous as it is common to take sitting fast on horseback for the whole art of horsemanship.

WILLIAM CAVENDISH, Duke of Newcastle

Soon as Aurora drives away the night
And edges eastern clouds with rosy light,
The healthy huntsman, with the cheerful horn,
Summons the dogs, and greets the dappled morn.
JOHN GAY

It is folly to take unwilling dogs out to hunt.
PLAUTUS

Everyone has observed how much more dogs are animated when they hunt in a pack, than when they pursue their game apart.
DAVID HUME

Like the athlete's exacting career, that of the fox-hound is a short one.
JOHN N.P. WATSON

The woods are made for the hunters of dreams,
The brooks for the fishers of song;
To the hunters who hunt for the gunless game
The streams and the woods belong.
> SAM WALTER FOSS
> 'The Bloodless Sportsman'

I remember how merry a start we got,
When the red fox broke from the gorse,
In a country so deep, with a scent so hot,
That the hound could outpace the horse.
> ADAM LINDSAY GORDON
> 'Ye Wearie Wayfarer'

Sottish drinking, indiscriminate gluttony, driving coaches, rustic sports such as fox-chases and horse-chases, are in my opinion infinitely below the honest and industrious professions of a tailor and shoemaker.
> LORD CHESTERFIELD

Yet if once we efface the joys of the chase
From the land, and outroot the Stud,
Good-bye to the Anglo-Saxon race!
Farewell to the Norman blood!
> ADAM LINDSAY GORDON
> 'Ye Wearie Wayfarer'

'Orses and dorgs is some men's fancy. They're wittles and drink to me – lodging wife and children – reading, writing, and 'rithmetic – snuff, tobacker and sleep.
> CHARLES DICKENS
> *David Copperfield*

One of his maxims was 'Don't marry for money but marry where money is', and he had carried this into effect ... thereby enabling his three sons to be brought up as keen fox-hunters, game-shooters, and salmon fishers.

> SIEGFRIED SASSOON
> *Memoirs of a Fox-Hunting Man*

The seat on a horse makes gentlemen of some and grooms of others.

> MIGUEL DE CERVANTES

It ar'nt that I loves the fox less, but that I loves the 'ound more.

> R.S. SURTEES
> *Handley Cross*

It ain't the 'unting as 'urts 'un, it's the 'ammer, 'ammer, 'ammer along the 'ard 'igh road.
PUNCH, 1856

Go anywhere in England, where there are natural, wholesome, contented and really nice English people; and what do you always find? That the stables are the real centre of the household.
GEORGE BERNARD SHAW
Heartbreak House

Whose only fit companion is his horse.
WILLIAM COWPER
Conversation

The Huntsman and Hounds. — Follow Pufs thro the Grounds.

He finds it hard without a pair
Of spectacles to shoot the hare.
The hare sits snug in leaves and grass,
And laughs to see the green man pass.
 HEINRICH HOFFMAN
  'The Man Who Went Out Shooting'

Deer walk upon our mountains, and the quail
Whistle about us their spontaneous cries.
  WALLACE STEVENS

My heart's in the Highlands, my heart is not here,
My heart's in the Highlands a-chasing the deer;
A-chasing the wild deer, a-chasing the roe,
My heart's in the Highlands wherever I go.
  ROBERT BURNS

He stands at bay,
And puts his last weak refuge in despair.
The big round tears run down his face;
He groans in anguish; while the growling pack,
Blood-happy, hang at his fair jutting chest,
And mark his beauteous chequered sides with gore.
  JAMES THOMPSON
  'Of a Stag'

How strange a thing is death, bringing to his knees,
    bringing to his antlers
The buck in the snow ...
Life, looking out attentive from the eyes of the doe.
    EDNA ST VINCENT MILLAY
    'The Buck in the Snow'

The first thing I saw in the morning ... was a group of five
stags, alert but unconcerned, staring from the primrose
bank just beyond the croft wall.
    GAVIN MAXWELL
    Ring of Bright Water

The stag at eve had drunk his fill,
Where danced the moon on Monan's rill,
And deep his midnight lair had made
In lone Glenartney's hazel shade.
    SIR WALTER SCOTT
    The Lady of the Lake

The huntsman repeated a cooing chant at the back of his nose ... with the names of hounds. They trotted with waving sterns, orderly and happy, enjoying the sounds, which to them were a promise of sport and fun.

    HENRY WILLIAMSON
    Tarka the Otter

The stream being narrow and shallow, the otter was given four minutes' law. Four minutes after Tarka had left he heard behind him the short and long notes of the horn, and the huntsman crying amidst the tongues of hounds.

    HENRY WILLIAMSON
    Tarka the Otter

The lovely sight of an otter moving with the stream, slowly, just touching with his feet, smooth as oil under the water. A twenty-pound dog, thought the Master, remaining quiet by the shallow water listening to the music of his hounds.

    HENRY WILLIAMSON
    Tarka the Otter

Walking is the favourite sport of the good and the wise.
> A.L. ROWSE
> *The Use of History*

I nauseate walking; 'tis a country diversion, I loathe the country.
> WILLIAM CONGREVE
> *The Way of The World*

I have no relish for the country; it is a kind of healthy grave.
> REVD SYDNEY SMITH
> in a letter to Miss G. Harcourt, 1838

All that unnecessary countryside.
> NOEL COWARD

Exercise is bunk. If you are healthy, you don't need it; if you are ill, you shouldn't take it.
> HENRY FORD

Sport is the preserver of health.
> HIPPOCRATES

Give me a clear blue sky over my head, and the green turf beneath my feet, a winding road before me, and a three hours' march to dinner – and then to thinking! It is hard if I cannot start some game on these lone heaths.
> WILLIAM HAZLITT
> *Table Talk*

If there is one word in the English language I hate, it is 'game'. It seems to imply that other creatures are about for our sport.

    ROBERT OTTAWAY

There's blood on the game you eat.

    CHARLES KINGSLEY

When a man wantonly destroys one of the works of man, we call him a vandal. When he wantonly destroys one of the works of God, we call him a sportsman.

    JOSEPH WOOD KRUTCH

Delightful task! to rear the tender thought,
To teach the young idea how to shoot.

    JAMES THOMSON

We were brought up to shoot, and by the curious paradox that those who are fondest of animals become, in such an environment, most bloodthirsty at a certain stage of their development, shooting occupied much of my time and thoughts during my school and university years.

    GAVIN MAXWELL
    Ring of Bright Water

A good marksman may miss.
PROVERB

Never shoot, never hit.
PROVERB

He that's always shooting must sometimes hit.
PROVERB

No shot is big enough to stop the target without hitting it.
A. BOGARDUS

You call pheasant shooting a sport, do you? Why? What is it? Up gets a guinea – off goes a penny-farthing – and, if you're lucky, down comes two-and-six! Bah!
PUNCH, 1889

It is a proverb in England that it is safer to shoot a man than a hare.

RALPH WALDO EMERSON

What he hit is history,
What he missed is mystery.

THOMAS HOOD

Regard shooting as a means to an end and not an end in itself.

JOHN MARCHINGTON

That men are clearly attracted by guns is beyond dispute; what is less clear is why.

JOHN MARCHINGTON

The fascination of shooting as a sport depends almost wholly on whether you are at the right or wrong end of a gun.

P.G. WODEHOUSE

The birds seem to consider the muzzle of my gun as their safest position.

REVD SYDNEY SMITH
Canon of St Paul's

A gun gives you the body, not the bird.
    HENRY DAVID THOREAU

Shooting gives me a good feeling. A lot of it is being together and friendly instead of feeling you are in some place where everybody hates you and wishes you ill. It is faster than baseball, and you are out on one strike.
    ERNEST HEMINGWAY
    quoted in *Portrait of Hemingway* by Lillian Ross

The art of shooting flying is arrived at tolerable perfection.
    The Sportsmen's Directory, 1792

There existed during my time at Oxford a curious clique of landed gentry so assertively un-urban that we affected a way of dressing quite unsuited to University life; at all times, for example, we wore tweed shooting suits and heavy shooting

shoes studded with nails and dull with dubbin, and at our heels trotted spaniels or Labrador retrievers.

> GAVIN MAXWELL
> *Ring of Bright Water*

The secret of straight shooting, like playing scratch golf, is constant practice, a steady temperament and a knowledge of the game.

> ROBERT CHURCHILL

Then another squadron of these racing, twisting, curling little birds is over us, and we are shooting as fast as we can load ... as I let off four barrels in scarcely more seconds, and as many partridges fly on unscathed.

> MAX HASTINGS

I like the power to shoot, even though I may not use it. The very perfection of our modern guns is to me one of their drawbacks; the use of them is so easy and so certain of effect that it takes away the romance of sport.

> RICHARD JEFFERIES

There is no one point in which the opinions of sportsmen are found to be more diametrically opposed to each other than in the size of shot to be used for shooting game.

> CAPTAIN LACY
> writing in 1842

The ideal shot picks out, well in front of him, the two leaders in a covey of partridges. They are almost certainly the old birds. If they are killed the covey will break up and spread to improve the breeding stock on the manor. The ideal shot never raises his gun to a low, probably immature, pheasant.

> MACDONALD HASTINGS
> *The Shotgun*

The gunmaker is something of a multiple personality at the best of times, for, in point of fact, an arm is seldom made by any one man. It is the work of barrel maker, lock maker, spring maker, stocker, mounter, engraver …

> HUGH B.C. POLLARD

> The Christmas cock-pheasant, he crows on the hill;
> His spurs are as javelins, as horn is his bill;
> A fox for fine cunning, he's brave to behold,
> A Syrian gleaming in purple and gold.
>> PATRICK CHALMERS

She became quite exceptional with a rifle, and bagged 964 stags on the Flemings' sporting estate at Black Mount in Argyll – a mere 36 short of the coveted four figures.

> OBITUARY OF JOAN FLEMING
> aunt by marriage of Peter and Ian Fleming
> *The Sunday Telegraph*, 1991

When flint-guns were the order of the day few sporting gentlemen of distinction ever thought of anything but the gun of a first-rate maker, for the simple reason that – on the *goodness of the work* depended the *quickness in firing*, and consequently the *filling of the bag*.

> Lt. Col. PETER HAWKER
> *Instructions to Young Sportsmen in All that Relates to Guns and Shooting*

The fitting of the stock of a gun to an individual is one of the highest arts of gunmaking.

> ROBERT CHURCHILL

If you call at Purdey's in South Audley Street in London's Mayfair today, they only need to know the number on the gun, anything from sixty to twenty-eight thousand, to tell you who bought it, the details of its measurements, the original choke in the barrels, and the precise date it was made.... It is still remarkable that you can often trace the history of London Best guns more exactly than the genealogical trees of their owners.

> MACDONALD HASTINGS
> *The Shotgun*

Those who shoot pheasants in England, or grouse in Scotland, or snipe in Ireland, speak in hushed tones when they mention partridge shooting in Spain. In the great rural wildernesses that still persist in the centre and south of the country, the wild partridges offer enthusiasts some of the highest, fastest, most challenging and exciting sport in the world.

    MAX HASTINGS

Hi! Handsome hunting man
Fire your little gun.
Bang!
Now the animal
Is dead and dumb and done
Nevermore to peep again, creep again, leap again
Eat or sleep or drink again, oh what fun.
    WALTER DE LA MARE
    'The Huntsman'

But He was never, well,
What I call
A sportsman;
For forty days
He went out into the desert
– And never shot anything.
    SIR OSBERT SITWELL

'Well, what sort of sport has Lord — had?'
    'Oh, the young Sahib shot divinely, but God was very merciful to the birds.'
    ANON

Unlike my predecessors, I have devoted more of my life to shunting and hooting than to hunting and shooting.
 SIR FRED BURROWS
 last governor of Bengal and former President of the
 National Union of Railwaymen

If one is shooting badly, one can sometimes conceal the fact beneath a lot of mumbling about 'two or three more down in that wood back there'.
 MAX HASTINGS

Up by candlelight again, and out till three, when the tide would no longer serve; but never had a chance as the geese

were too much persecuted to venture near the shore, and
the sea too rough to come near them afloat.

    LT. COL. PETER HAWKER
    Diaries

Godfrey Webb went out duck shooting. When asked
afterwards if he had shot any, 'Not even a Mallard
Imaginaire' was his answer.

    MAURICE BARING
    The Puppet Show of Memory, 1922

In Britain we are more fortunate than most in the number
and variety of geese which winter on our shores and inland
waters.

    ERIC BEGBIE

The fowler's world of remote and windswept estuaries
where geese and duck feed, where waders bustle and fill the
air with their plaintive music, is one which has inspired

artists and writers for centuries. The wildfowler is a lucky man and he knows it.

DAVID S.P. CANT

Wildfowling is the pursuit of wild fowl in wild places. Wildfowling is a ragged skein of Greylag battling against a howling gale in a December dawn as dark clouds skud across a lightening sky. Wildfowling is the whistle of Widgeon, barely visible under a waning moon.

ERIC BEGBIE
Modern Wildfowling

The true philosopher of the gun is the wildfowler, for he must have the sensitive eye of an artist, a love of solitude and lonely places. He measures beauty by the flash of a bird's wing, by the glint of dawn sun on sliding waters, by the march of slow clouds. He is the son of solitude, the lonely one.

J. WENTWORTH DAY

I ranged o 'er the fields from morn until night,
My dog and my gun my constant delight.
CAPTAIN LACY
writing in 1842

The ability [of a retriever] to withstand severe cold is essential and on several occasions I have witnessed my own labradors emerge from the water on a winter's morning and literally turn white with frost within a few minutes.

ERIC BEGBIE
Modern Wildfowling

The labour of working the fowl was an odd mixture of ecstasy and slavery.

COL. PETER HAWKER

No wildfowler should proceed out unless accompanied by a trained retrieving dog and that, once on the saltings, he should shoot at nothing which he, his family or his friends will not eat.

ERIC BEGBIE
Modern Wildfowling

Hawks are right nervous and they've got fantastic eye-sight, and things are ten times worse for them than they are for us. So you've to be right patient, an' all t'time you're walking her you've to talk to her, all soft like, like you do to a baby.

BARRY HINES
Kes

– In behint yon auld fail dyke
I wot there lies a new-slain knight;
And naebody kens that he lies there
But his hawk, his hound, and his lady fair.

His hound is to the hunting gane,
His hawk to fetch the wild-fowl hame;
His lady's ta'en anither mate,
So we may make our dinner sweet.

BALLAD
'The Twa Corbies'

Turning and turning in the widening gyre
The falcon cannot hear the falconer.
W.B. YEATS
'The Second Coming'

What I like about it is its shape; it's so beautifully proportioned. The neat head, the way the wings fold over on its back. Its tail, just the right length, and that down on the thighs, just like a pair of plus-fours.
BARRY HINES
Kes

See! from the brake the whirring pheasant springs,
And mounts exulting on triumphant wings:
Short is his joy; he feels the fiery wound,
Flutters in blood, and panting beats the ground.
ALEXANDER POPE
'Windsor Forest'

I'd sooner, except the penalties, kill a man than a hawk.
ROBINSON JEFFERS

A hound and hawk no longer shall be tokens of
    disaffection.
A cockfight shall cease,
To be a breach of the peace,
And a horse-race an insurrection.
    ANON, *c.*1700

Walpole ... even when Prime Minister was said to open his
gamekeeper's letters first of the batch.
    G.M. TREVELYAN

Ever since (and possibly before) D.H. Lawrence immor-
talised the gamekeeper, ladies have liked them a lot ... As a
result many gentlemen say that if they were not gentlemen
they would have liked to be gamekeepers.
    DOUGLAS SUTHERLAND
    The English Gentleman's Wife

Men are generally more careful of the breed of their horses
and dogs than of their children.
    WILLIAM PENN
    'Some Fruits of Solitude', in *Reflections and Maxims
    Relating to the Conduct of Human Life*, 1693

The British are a horsy people.
    R.W.F. POOLE

Some squire, perhaps, you take delight to rack; ...
Makes love with nods, and knees beneath a table;
Whose laughs are hearty, though his jests are coarse,
And loves you best of all things – but his horse.
    ALEXANDER POPE

The gentleman must realize that once he is in the saddle he must be as rude as possible to anyone who crosses his path.

DOUGLAS SUTHERLAND
The English Gentleman

It's a most uncommonly cramping thing ... to sit on horseback and look over the hedges at the wrong thing, and not be able to put your hand to make it right. What people do who go into politics I can't think: it drives me almost mad to see mismanagement over only a few hundred acres.

GEORGE ELIOT
Middlemarch

She enjoyed having people to stay at her family home, Barton Abbey near Steeple Aston, especially her competitors, and she loved to talk horses after dinner in the panelled dining room with its splendid trophies.

MURIEL BOWEN on Joan Fleming

He told me afterwards that there were two things which he wished at that moment: either that the race was all over, or that something would happen to prevent it taking place at all. It is sometimes forgotten that without such feelings heroism could not exist.

SIEGFRIED SASSOON
Memoirs of a Fox-Hunting Man

When I appear in public people expect me to neigh, grind my teeth, paw the ground and swish my tail – none of which is easy.

THE PRINCESS ROYAL

There is no secret so close as that between a rider and his horse.

> R.S. SURTEES
> *Mr Sponge's Sporting Tour*

I don't even like *old* cars ... I'd rather have a goddam horse. A horse is at least *human*.

> J.D. SALINGER
> *The Catcher in the Rye*

Well did not that great man, I think that it was Sir Walter Scott, but if it warn't, 'twas little Bartley, the bootmaker, say, that there was no young man wot would not rather have a himputation on his morality than on his 'ossmanship.

> R.S. SURTEES
> *Handley Cross*

> Better to hunt in fields, for health unbought,
> Than fee the doctor for a nauseous draught.
> The wise, for cure, on exercise depend;
> God never made his work for man to mend.
> JOHN DRYDEN
> 'Epistle to John Driden of Chesterton', 1700

The outside of a horse is good for the inside of a man.

> LT. COL. HARRY LLEWELLYN

We attended stables, as we attended church, in our best clothes, thereby no doubt showing the degree of respect due to horses, as to the deity.

> SIR OSBERT SITWELL

Horseback Hall, consisting of a prison for the horses with an annexe for the ladies and gentlemen who rode them; hunted them, talked about them, bought them and sold them, and gave nine tenths of their lives to them.
GEORGE BERNARD SHAW

Did you know horses lead to divorces? You've no idea how sexually promiscuous they are in the shires. It's all that jumping up and down on horses that does it. They get over-stimulated.
LORD ARRAN

You may have my husband but not my horse.
D.H. LAWRENCE
Kangaroo

It's awfully bad luck on Diana,
Her ponies have swallowed their bits;
She fished down their throats with a spanner
And frightened them all into fits.
> JOHN BETJEMAN
> 'Hunter Trials'

It was a glorious sight, and the come-and-go of the little
quick hooves, and the incessant salutations of ponies that
had met before ... were enough to drive a four-footed thing
wild.
> RUDYARD KIPLING
> *The Maltese Cat*

Frightful rows go on in Palm Beach because the women are
all pinching their husbands' horses.
> JILLY COOPER
> *Horsie*

Nobody has any right to go round looking like a horse and
behaving as if it was all right. You don't catch horses going
round looking like people, do you?
> DOROTHY PARKER

In the winter I simply live in the stable.
> MARY DEWHURST
> *Conversation With a Friend*, 1941

I say to parents, especially wealthy parents, 'Don't give your
son money. As far as you can afford it, give him horses'.
> WINSTON CHURCHILL
> *My Early Life*

A horse is dangerous at both ends and uncomfortable in the middle.

> IAN FLEMING
> *Sunday Times*, 9 October 1966

Haig, where are you riding to? Don't ask me, ask the horse.

> SIGMUND FREUD

To confess that you are totally Ignorant about the Horse, is social suicide: you will be despised by everybody, especially the horse.

> W.C. SELLAR & R.J. YEATMAN
> *Horse Nonsense*

It takes a good deal of physical courage to ride a horse. This, however, I have. I get it at about forty cents a flask, and take it as required.

> STEPHEN LEACOCK
> *Reflections on Riding*

My friend, judge not me,
Thou seest I judge not thee.
Betwixt the stirrup and the ground
Mercy I asked, and mercy found.
> WILLIAM CAMDEN
> epitaph for a man killed by falling from his horse

'Horse driving' (which is its official British Horse Society title) is the fastest growing equestrian sport.
> R.W.F. POOLE

A competition carriage....carries four: the driver, the umpire and two grooms. (Should a carriage turn over at speed, expert and urgent assistance is needed to sort out the tangle of legs, bodies and harness.)
> R.W.F. POOLE

What an amazing sensation it is to be perched up there, looking down on those four surging, muscular, sinewy backs; to smell that marvellous brew of horse, sweat and

leather. But most amazing of all were the signals coming down the reins – the feeling of strength and power and suppressed speed.

    R.W.F. POOLE

Ay, they heard his foot upon the stirrup,
And the sound of iron on stone,
And how the silence surged softly backward,
When the plunging hoofs were gone.
    WALTER DE LA MARE
    'The Listeners'

I sprang to the stirrup, and Joris, and he;
I galloped, Dirck galloped, we galloped all three.
    ROBERT BROWNING
    'How They Brought the Good News from Ghent to
    Aix'

The men of the Golden Horde were almost as kind to children as to horses – though naturally they regarded them with less reverence.

    SIR OSBERT SITWELL
    The Scarlet Tree

Alas! what boots it that my noble steed,
Chosen so carefully, the field outran?
I did not reckon, bookie, on *your* speed:
The proper study of mankind is man.
    GEORGE ROSTREVOR HAMILTON
    'On a Distant Prospect of an Absconding Bookmaker'

I have seen flowers come in stony places
And kind things done by men with ugly faces,
And the gold cup won by the worst horse at the races,
So I trust, too.
JOHN MASEFIELD
'Epilogue'

There is a glare in some men's eyes which seems to say, 'Beware, I am dangerous; *Noli me tangere.*' Lord Brougham's face has this. A mischievous excitability is the most obvious expression of it. If he were a horse, nobody would buy him; with that eye no one could answer for his temper.

> WALTER BAGEHOT
> *Biographical Studies*

Give a man a horse he can ride,
Give a man a boat he can sail.

> JAMES THOMSON
> 'Sunday up the River'

Ready to race, though blown, though beat,
As long as his will could lift his feet;
Ready to burst his heart to pass
Each gasping horse in that street of grass.

> JOHN MASEFIELD
> 'Right Royal'

She raced at the rasper, I felt my knees grasp her,
I found my hands give to her strain on the bit,
She rose when The Clown did – our silks as we bounded
Brush'd lightly, our stirrups clash'd loud as we lit.

> ADAM LINDSAY GORDON
> 'How We Beat the Favourite', *A Lay of the Loamshire
> Hunt Cup*

God never did make a more calm, quiet, innocent recreation than angling.

> IZAAK WALTON
> *The Compleat Angler*

No life so happy and so pleasant, as the life of a well governed Angler; for when the Lawyer is swallowed up with business, and the Statesman is preventing or contriving plots, then we sit on Cowslip-banks, hear the birds sing, and possess our selves in as much quietness as these silent silver streams, which we now see glide so quietly by us.

> IZAAK WALTON
> *The Compleat Angler*

And angling too, that solitary vice,
Whatever Izaak Walton sings or says:
The quaint, old, cruel coxcomb, in his gullet
Should have a hook, and a small trout to pull it.
>LORD BYRON
>*Don Juan*

Fish die belly upwards and rise to the surface. It is their way
of falling.
>ANDRÉ GIDE
>*Journals*, 1939–50

El pez muere por la boca. The fish dies because he opens his
mouth.
>SPANISH PROVERB

I may be wrong, but I don't think there has ever been any
anti-blood sports demonstration against angling.
>MILES KINGTON
>*Punch*, 22 May 1972

No human being, however great, or powerful, was ever so
free as a fish.
>JOHN RUSKIN
>*The Two Paths*

The only difficult thing about dry-fly-fishing is finding an
opportunity to practise it.
>RICHARD WALKER
>*Dick Walker's Angling*

I love any discourse of rivers, and fish and fishing.
> IZAAK WALTON
> *The Compleat Angler*

Evening and the first hour of darkness, is the most important time of all for the angler.
> PETER WHEAT

Angling may be said to be so like the mathematics that it can never be fully learnt.
> IZAAK WALTON
> *The Compleat Angler*

And nigh the toppling reed, still as death
The great pike lies, the murderous patriarch.
EDMUND BLUNDEN
'The Pike'

Never forget that only dead fish swim with the stream.
MALCOLM MUGGERIDGE

Has it ever struck you that the trouts bite best on the
Sabbath? God's critters tempting decent men.
J.M. BARRIE

Fly fishing may be a very pleasant amusement; but angling
or float fishing I can only compare to a stick and a string,
with a worm at one end and a fool at the other.
SAMUEL JOHNSON

The rewards of big catches and heavy fish are possible only
through dedicated effort.
ANON.

For the price of a pint I've gained all sorts of invaluable help
from those connected with a fishery.
PETER WHEAT

Then there was the case of the pike that swallowed a live
rat which tried to gnaw its way out of the pike's stomach. It
had got as far as its shoulders, with its head projecting out
of the pike, when the pike took an angler's spoon and was
caught.
RICHARD WALKER
Dick Walker's Angling

As no man is born an artist, so no man is born an angler.
    IZAAK WALTON
    The Compleat Angler

Fishing is undoubtedly a form of madness but, happily for the once-bitten, there is no cure.
    SIR ALEC DOUGLAS-HOME

The charm of fishing is that it is the pursuit of what is elusive but obtainable, a perpetual series of occasions for hope.
    JOHN BUCHAN

I suppose that nowhere else, and never before, have so many large fish been caught on such fine tackle and small hooks, as have been caught on the best dry fly rivers in recent years ... The chief point is to keep below the fish, and fight always with the stream helping you.
    VISCOUNT GREY OF FALLODEN
    Fly Fishing

I never lost a little fish. Yes I am free to say
It always was the biggest fish I caught that got away.
    EUGENE FIELD

Many things are taught at public schools, but Winchester is
probably the only school at which the most scientific and
highly developed form of angling can be learnt.
    VISCOUNT GREY OF FALLODEN
    Fly Fishing

We catched fish and talked, and we took a swim now and
then to keep off sleepiness. We had mighty good weather as
a general thing, and nothing ever happened to us at all.
    MARK TWAIN

Only the gamefish swims upstream.
> JOHN TROTWOOD MOORE
> *The Unafraid*

> Immense, of fishy form and mind,
> Squamous, omnipotent, and kind;
> And under that Almighty Fin
> The littlest fish may enter in.
> Oh! never fly conceals a hook,
> Fish say, in the Eternal Brook,
> But more than mundane weeds are there,
> And mud, celestially fair.
> > RUPERT BROOKE
> > 'Heaven'

Try hard to find the fish by all the ways you can think of, because it is by far the most important thing in fishing. Nothing else matters until you've done all you can to find where the fish are.
> RICHARD WALKER
> *Dick Walker's Angling*

With a very large fish – the thought of losing which is really dreadful – I always have a secret fear of getting the net ready too soon, lest the act should be noticed by some unseen influence, and treated as a sign of that pride which deserves a fall.

>VISCOUNT GREY OF FALLODEN
>*Fly Fishing*

I had always wanted to visit New Zealand ever since my father, who had once been commander of the battlecruiser *New Zealand*, had told me of the marvellous trout fishing he had enjoyed when the ship had paid a visit there.

>LUDOVIC KENNEDY

One piece of advice may be given to all anglers, who begin dry fly fishing when they are young, and that is to make themselves ambidextrous, to be able to cast with the left hand as well as with the right.

>VISCOUNT GREY OF FALLODEN
>*Fly Fishing*

How then does one 'spot' fish ...? First, one needs the best available polarized glasses to remove surface glare from the water. Secondly, sunlight and still or reasonably gentle conditions are desirable.

>JOHN ENGLAND
>*Black Gnat*

Learning to cast a fly is not always easy, nor is learning to spot fish. It is worth the effort nevertheless.

>JOHN ENGLAND
>*Black Gnat*

I am satiated with fishing stories – there's no truth in them! The man who caught that fish (stuffed in a glass case) is a blasted liar!

> GEORGE ROBEY
> *In Conversation after a Piscatorial Society Dinner*

It is astonishing how soon the exact position of one rising trout will be taken by another as soon as there is a vacancy: sometimes if the angler gets a trout quickly down stream after hooking it, he may on returning to the place after the first trout has been landed, find a second already occupying the vacant place and feeding there, as if it had known the advantages of this particular spot.

> VISCOUNT GREY OF FALLODEN
> *Fly Fishing*

Nothing quite compares with the sight of a large fish rising, 'head and shoulders' above the surface, to take a dry fly in perfect weather and water conditions.

> JOHN ENGLAND
> *Black Gnat*

Dr Strabismus (Whom God Preserve) of Utrecht is carrying out research work with a view to crossing salmon with mosquitoes. He says it will mean a bite every time for fishermen.

> J.B. MORTON

What a day! Two salmon this morning, and the offer of the Exchequer this afternoon.

> NEVILLE CHAMBERLAIN
> in a letter declining office, May 1923

Every professional or business person has times when the pressures of modern life seem insufferable ... One morning ... as I joined the city-bound traffic, my nervous system suddenly snapped. I should be fishing.

> JOHN ENGLAND
> *Black Gnat*

Overwork, n. A dangerous disorder affecting high public functionaries who want to go fishing.

> AMBROSE BIERCE
> *The Devil's Dictionary*

Weirpools, where the air is full of exciting noises as the river works through the systems and falls in crazed heaps of whiteness from the gates into the pools below, have a very special appeal, and who among anglers could fail to ... think of the monstrous fish which inhabit such places.

> PETER WHEAT

A man may fish with the worm that hath eat of a king, and eat of the fish that hath fed of that worm.

> WILLIAM SHAKESPEARE
> *Hamlet*

That is no country for old men. The young
In one another's arms, birds in the trees
– Those dying generations – at their song,
The salmon-falls, the mackerel-crowded seas,
Fish, flesh, or fowl, commend all summer long.

> W.B. YEATS
> 'The Tower'

Each angler will create his personal angling world in which
only he can dwell.
PETER WHEAT

Then may you safely strike and hold him short,
And at your will, prolong or end your sport.
JOHN DENNYS
The Secrets of Angling, 1613

The fish long playing with the baited hook
At last is caught.
PHINEAS FLETCHER
1633

Experience is my master, and angling my exercise.
RICHARD FRANCK

The fish will soon be caught that nibbles at every bait.
THOMAS FULLER

The end of fishing is not angling, but catching.
THOMAS FULLER

It is rare to find a fish that will not some time or other bite.
THOMAS FULLER

If or chance or hunger's powerful sway
Directs the roving trout this fatal way.
He greedily sucks in the twining bait
And toys and nibbles the fallacious meat.
JOHN GAY

The line with its rod is a long instrument whose lesser end holds a small reptile while the other is held by a great fool.
FRANÇOIS GUYET

The fish adores the bait.
GEORGE HERBERT

You must lose a fly to catch a trout.
GEORGE HERBERT

A woman who has never seen her husband fishing doesn't know what a patient man she has married.
EDGAR HOWE

A thoughtful wife is one who has a juicy steak ready when her husband returns from a day's fishing.
ANON.

Does the chairman of an angling club ever use his casting vote?

COLIN M. JARMAN

Fishing is a laborious way of taking it easy.

FRANKLIN P. JONES

Well, I have fished and caught a frog; brought little to pass with as much ado.

BISHOP HUGH LATIMER

The trout makes the angler the most gentlemanly and readiest sport of all other fishes.

WILLIAM LAUSON

It has to be observed that angling is the name given to fishing by people who can't fish.

STEPHEN LEACOCK

What is emphatic in angling is made so by the long silences
– the unproductive periods.
    THOMAS McGUANE
    Essays on Sport

Fishing is a delusion entirely surrounded by liars in old
clothes.
    DON MARQUIS

It is a great pleasure for a man sometime to take with his
angle a dish of fish in those waters where fish is plenty and
well-preserved and not use any other engines but with the
hook.
    LEONARD MARSHALL
    writing in 1599

A trout is a fish known mainly by hearsay. It lives on
anything not included in a fisherman's equipment.
    H.I. PHILLIPS

Moonlight may be magic to some people but it holds no magic for fishers.

SIDNEY SPENCER

Bragging may not bring happiness, but no man having caught a large fish goes home through an alley.

ANON.

Caution is the most valuable asset in angling, especially if you are the fish.

ANON.

There are two types of fisherman – those who fish for sport and those who fish for fish.

ANON.

Most people who do great things are alone, especially on a river bank.

ANON.

An angler eats more than he gets.

PROVERB

The curious thing about fishing is you never want to go home. If you catch anything, you can't stop. If you don't catch anything, you hate to leave in case something might bite.

GLADYS TABER

There are two periods when fishing is good – before you get there and after you leave.

ANON.

Nothing grows faster than a fish from the time it bites until he gets away.

ANON.

Many fishermen catch their fish by the tale.

ANON.

Truth is when one fisherman calls another fisherman a liar.

ANON.

The best fish swim near the bottom.
PROVERB

The Gods do not deduct from man's allotted span the hours spent in fishing.
BABYLONIAN PROVERB
often quoted by Herbert Hoover

If you wish to be happy forever, learn to fish.
CHINESE PROVERB

It is ill fishing if the hook is bare.
SCOTTISH PROVERB

Fishing differs from all other sports in one essential detail; it is the only sport, in which the quarry has to co-operate and play its own active and willing part.
VIVIAN BAILEY

Fishing, if I, a fisher, may protest,
of pleasures is the sweetest, of sports the best,
Of exercises the most excellent;
Of recreations the most innocent;
But now the sport is marred, and wot you why?
Fishes decrease, and fishers multiply.
>THOMAS BASTARD
>1598

The Salmon is the most stately fish that any man may angle
to in fresh water.
>DAME JULIANA BERNERS
>prioress (1343–1443)

Unfading moths, immortal flies,
And the worm that never dies.
And in that Heaven of all their wish,
There shall be no more land, say fish.
>RUPERT BROOKE
>'Heaven'

The weather for catching fish is that weather, and no other,
in which fish are caught.
>WILLIAM BLAKE

Lays down his rod, and takes his line in hand.
And by degrees, getting the fish to land.
>WILLIAM BROWNE
>1613

Trouts are tickled best in muddy water.
>SAMUEL BUTLER

Catching salmon in Britain is not a sport, it is an art.
PETER CHIPPENHAM

They thought best fishing still in troubled streams.
SIR WILLIAM DAVENANT

Fortunately angling is not a glamorous sport where 'stars' are manufactured overnight. It is essentially for the practical, a sport where respect must be earned the hard way – by results.
PETER MASKELL

It [angling] is an employment for my idle time, which is then not idly spent.
SIR HENRY WOTTON

Angling is somewhat like poetry, men are to be born so.
IZAAK WALTON
The Compleat Angler

Someone just back of you while you are fishing is as bad as someone looking over your shoulder while you write a letter to your girl.
ERNEST HEMINGWAY

Still fishes he that catches one.
DELAMOTHES
1592

All rods can catch fish: their success depends on the hand that uses them.
CHARLES RITZ

No one ever did consistently well with unsuitable tackle.
SIDNEY SPENCER

Fly rods are like women; they won't play if they are maltreated.
CHARLES RITZ

A good rod is, without doubt, the Angler's chief requisite.
Hardy Brothers Catalogue, 1866

The Court of King George V was not renowned for its interest in literature. When leading novelist Thomas Hardy died in 1928, one courtier was heard to say, 'Old Hardy's dead. We must send a telegram.'

Next day, fishing rod maker to the Royal Family (Mr Hardy of Alnwick, Northumberland) was surprised to see a telegram from his Sovereign condoling with the family on his death.

He was the only Hardy that the Court had ever heard of.
ANON.

Our soft grass and mild climate has enabled us to foster new sports ... particularly cricket – a game which the English, not being a spiritual people, have invented in order to give themselves some conception of eternity.

    LORD MANCROFT
    Bees in Some Bonnets

Cricket is not in reality a very popular game in England.

    GEORGE ORWELL

Cricket is of the very soul of England.

    THE CHURCH TIMES

Villagers do not think village cricket is funny.

    JOHN ARLOTT

I would rather see the whole village dead at my feet than a man bowling in braces.

    ADRIAN ALLINGTON

Real old-fashioned village cricket is a serious matter for the villager and immense fun for the visitor.

    IAN PEEBLES

Village cricket spread fast through the land. In those days, before it became scientific, cricket was the best game in the world to watch – each ball a potential crisis.

    G.M. TREVELYAN

It's a funny kind of month, October. For the really keen cricket fan it's when you discover that your wife left you in May.

    DENIS NORDEN
    She Magazine, October 1977

My wife had an uncle who could never walk down the nave of his abbey without wondering whether it would take a spin.

    SIR ALEC DOUGLAS-HOME

Many continentals think life is a game, the English think cricket is a game.

    GEORGE MIKES

If the French were to play cricket they would all want to be 'batsmen' – the cynosure of all eyes – at the same time, just as nearly all of them want to be Prime Minister.

    JEAN FAYARD

I have always looked on cricket as organised loafing.

    WILLIAM TEMPLE
    when Headmaster of Repton

Joan's mother, Lady Hunloke ... played spirited cricket ... Joan in turn proved a useful bat and delighted to recall of one well-struck boundary: 'The ball went into Lady

Baldwin's long skirts and the chaps were so laid back looking for it that it was an age before the ball was back in play.'

OBITUARY OF JOAN FLEMING
aunt by marriage of Peter and Ian Fleming
Sunday Telegraph, 1991

Ideally, the umpire should combine the integrity of a Supreme Court justice, the physical agility of an acrobat, the endurance of Job and the imperturbability of Buddha.

TIME, 25 August 1961

His off drives are like a white owl flying.

NEVILLE CARDUS
Days in the Sun

Whenever a Hambledon man made a good hit with four or five runs, you could hear the deep mouths of the whole multitude baying away in pure Hampshire.

JOHN N. NYREN

The very names of cricket bat and ball make English fingers tingle.

> WILLIAM HAZLITT

During his first few overs Grace's bat was like a stout door bolted against evil; he watched every ball as though Satan were behind it.

> NEVILLE CARDUS

Now in Maytime to the wicket
Out I march with bat and pad;
See the son of grief at cricket
Trying to be glad.

> A.E. HOUSMAN
> 'Reveille'

There's a breathless hush in the Close to-night –
Ten to make and the match to win –
A bumping pitch and a blinding light,
An hour to play and the last man in.
And it's not for the sake of a ribboned coat,
Or the selfish hope of a season's fame,
But his Captain's hand on his shoulder smote –
'Play up! play up! and play the game!'

> SIR HENRY NEWBOLT
> 'Vitai Lampada'

While they were content to peck cautiously at the ball, he never spared himself in his efforts to do it a violent injury.

> P.G. WODEHOUSE
> *Chester Forgets Himself*

There was ease in Casey's manner as he stepped into his
  place,
There was pride in Casey's bearing, and a smile on
  Casey's face,
And when, responding to the cheers, he lightly doffed
  his hat,
No stranger in the crowd could doubt 'twas Casey at the
  bat.
  ERNEST LAWRENCE THAYER

Cricket civilizes people and creates good gentlemen.
  ROBERT MUGABE